Praise For......
Money NOW Safely: Your Financial Gap

"This book covers the necessary, but rarely used steps to safely making money. Each section of the book contains 'action steps' which helped me employ each method to free myself financially, something only expensive courses usually use, so this book is great value for money. It also contains great resources such as tools to work out retirement income, which I found very comforting and motivating. Invaluable book for the money! 5 stars!" – *Ollie Vinton*

"This book is short and sweet, but to the point. It made me very aware of what I need to do and how I can prepare for my retirement and financial future. I recommend reading this book - it's a quick and easy read and will certainly help you plan for your future! The author made the content very easy to understand and provided very useful information on the best way to optimize your money." – *Nicole MacDonald*

"Concise and motivational inspiration and advice to get started wisely and safely on a plan to meet my income needs by retirement. Just what I was looking for!" – *Leslie Jordan*

MONEY NOW SAFELY: YOUR FINANCIAL GAP

#1 OF 8 STEPS GUARANTEED TO HELP YOU INCREASE CASH, ELIMINATE DEBT, RETIRE WEALTHY AND ENJOY LIFE

Gail Nichols

Fort Lauderdale, Florida

Significant discounts for bulk sales are available.
Email: GNichols@SafeWealthCreation.com

TABLE OF CONTENTS

Introduction

I want to thank you and congratulate you for purchasing this book, *"Money NOW Safely: Your Financial Gap. #1 of 8 Steps Guaranteed to Help You Increase Cash, Eliminate Debt, Retire Wealthy and Enjoy Life"*.

This book contains proven steps and strategies on how to achieve financial freedom starting NOW in order to accomplish your dreams for you and your family.

Are you an entrepreneur, manager or rising star in your company? ......

Do you want to enjoy a fun lifestyle today and also provide for your future but you're worried about losing your savings?

If you see older people working way past their retirement date and hope that won't be you or if you're not sure how to make the right choices to organize your finances or even if you don't know what the right questions are to ask to become financially independent.... Then this book is a must read for you.

If you're tired of reading about hot investment tips and get-rich-quick formulas that sound too good to be true and maybe actually tried a few yourself and got burned...

You will find my recommendations in this book to be open, honest and realistically achievable.

This book removes all the intimidating barriers and tactics of conventional financial advice.

It's **Step #1** in a series of *Money NOW Safely* books that lead you through the 8 proven, easy and simple steps to achieve financial freedom without stress and pressure.

This will help you improve the **quality** of your life now and in the future with small, realistic and achievable changes in your life that you can stick to without suffering.

Creating safe money habits are effective because they take little time and effort and yet lead you to impressive and satisfying results over time.

For example, in this book you'll learn the **major problem that 96 percent of people have** that prevents them from becoming financially secure...and they don't even know they have it!

Naturally, the sooner you identify a problem...the easier it is to fix it!

We'll examine this problem and what impact solving it will have on improving your life and lifestyle to help you achieve your goals for increasing cash, eliminating debt, retiring wealthy and enjoying life more abundantly along the way.

You'll learn about an **ancient and still relevant math rule** that affects every aspect of your financial health. Without knowing this rule and applying it wisely, research shows your likelihood of achieving financial security are almost zero.

Fortunately, this book and the others in the series of *Money NOW Safely* books are designed to bring you up to speed quickly.

If you haven't yet read **Step #2 – Get: Money NOW Safely: Ka-Ching! (By Gail Nichols)** on **Amazon.com** or via **MoneyNowSafely.com** and **SafeWealthCreation.com**

Thank you for purchasing this book. I hope you enjoy it!

About The Author

Hi! I'm Gail Nichols

Like you, I want to enjoy life today and in the future, with enough money to sustain me comfortably on my life's journey, without being a burden to my family and friends.

I've learned a lot during my 35+ years' earning money and investing it various ways with mixed results. I want to share my lessons with you to help you avoid wasting time, money and heartache along the way.

Firstly, here's a bit about me so you know where I'm coming from.

Originally, I graduated as a Registered Nurse and specialized in neurosurgery (brain surgery) in the operating room of the Hospital for Sick Children. Wanting to broaden my knowledge and experience, I ventured into the business world, which continues to be challenging and inspiring.

I became a successful realtor, bank manager, stockbroker, independent financial services provider and business owner. I co-founded an international telecommunications company together with my husband and business partner, Richard Cherry, who created and patented numerous innovative products and services used worldwide today.

Richard and I experienced the financial challenges of creating and funding businesses from scratch and growing them. We were honored with a **Smithsonian Computerworld Award** and **President's Task Force Award** for patenting the business method and software for the original virtual call center which consequently enabled meaningful home-based employment for over 25 thousand people in the USA, Canada and the U.K. That company we named Willow CSN is now Arise.com.

The lessons we have learned also apply to you entrepreneurs, managers and rising stars who wish to enjoy your lifestyle today as well as provide a solid and safe foundation for your future.

Thank You for your interest!

   www.MoneyNowSafely.com

The Money NOW Safely Solution

In this book, you'll learn stuff that will amaze, shock and surprise you. You'll learn about money; numerous critical facts you may not know.

But, what you *do* with what you learn will determine your future.

It's simple stuff wealthy people do every day.

Conventional financial advice is flawed because even if you commit to taking the first few steps and start seeing small results, it's often hard to stay on track long term.

"Saving Money" rarely leads to long-term financial security that lasts through retirement because it creates a lot of stress, unrealistic expectations and even a feeling of helplessness.

This is because conventional saving programs don't address the underlying causes of lack of financial independence. They depend on people getting to a point where they say they "have to save something", and start to change their life but this only lasts until that short burst of motivation dies out.

If you can relate to this very common and infuriating savings cycle, then you're in the right place!

The most important thing to realize is that being broke isn't your fault. Everybody is simply a result of his or her environment and experience.

If you're tired of your current environment's poor effect on your financial, emotional and physical health and if you're looking for a simple and sustainable method to achieve your financial goals without having to jump through crazy hoops, then you are in the right place.

This book is not another "fad savings" program. We are focused on helping you change your current financial habits into better ones in order to see sustainable results and skyrocket you towards your goals.

Shall we get started?

Let's Get Started...

First things first: **CONGRATULATIONS!**

Starting this book is a bold first step to becoming financially independent and I'm proud to say you're not alone in that journey.

You're joining a thriving group of thousands of successful folks that I have coached over many years and I'm here to support you along the way.

Whether you are an entrepreneur, manager or rising star looking to live the lifestyle of your dreams by being financially secure, THANK YOU for purchasing this book.

So let's go ahead and learn some of the easy ways to increase your cash, eliminate your debt and save money to replace your future salary, business or career income when you retire.

At that point, you do not NEED to work any longer.

You may CHOOSE to work – but you don't NEED to work.

That's Financial Independence – where your dreams actually *can* come true.

Would you like to know how to get there as soon as possible?

Okay, let's look at a sobering statistic you need to take into account..

Yikes! Say It Ain't So...

Here's a sobering statistic from the U.S. Government:

Out of 100 people turning age 65 today ......

Only 4 are financially secure.

Imagine being at retirement age but unable to stop working because you're one of the 96 of 100 who haven't saved enough money to supplement your pension income.

Instead, you have 3 choices:

1) **Rely on charity**. (Not a pleasant thought)
2) **Move back in with your kids.** (BONUS: if you have more than 1 child, you have choices ☺)
3) **Keep working until the day you drop.** (You probably see this happening every day.)

However, if you'd rather be free to travel, relax with your friends and family without worrying about debt and income, there are easy-to-apply solutions which we will cover in this series of books.

There's a secret to having Money NOW Safely, which I will reveal to you as we work through this and the other related books together.

However, once you learn this secret, you need to apply it to your life for the magic to happen.

My mission is to be a resource to help you become financially independent with TAX-FREE income for life THAT YOU CANNOT OUTLIVE.

So congrats on taking the plunge! I can't wait to see your progress.

Action Step:

Identify the financial goals you want to achieve and determine to start NOW to reach them.

May I Be Bold?

Let's get right to the point!

In this book, you'll learn stuff that will amaze, shock and surprise you. You just saw a preview.

I'm here to teach you about money. Numerous critical facts you may not know.

What people DO with what they learn will determine their future.

Sadly, without applying what you learn in this course, the perilous path to poverty becomes inevitable for that 96 percent of us.

If you delay implementation of what you learn in this book, there's a 96 percent chance it will never happen, in spite of your good intentions.

We're going create a realistic Game Plan in this series of **Money NOW Safely** books.

We'll figure out where you are today and where you want to be in the future and what's going to have to happen along the way.

We'll be tweaking things as we go along so they keep pace with your individual lifestyle.

So we're going to be always inspecting what you expect.

Action Step:

If you choose to work together with us to improve your financial security, we promise to help you and your family achieve your goals safely.

The first step is to request your free **No-Obligation Analysis** by completing and submitting the form at the end of this book on page "A".

FINANCIAL FREEDOM

Wendy's Story

Remember that statistic about 96 percent of people age 65 being unable to afford to stop working?

I was in Wendy's not long ago and had an experience that I won't forget.

I was sitting at a table drinking my coffee and checking emails on my smartphone when I saw a staffer in uniform cleaning tables nearby. I was surprised at her apparent age since she seemed to be around my Mom's age (who is vibrant at 89 years!)

I thought, "Wow! They sure are hiring staff *really* senior these days!"

But, then I thought maybe she's just looking for a way to stay busy and earn a few extra dollars. Still, it's hard being on your feet all day at that age.

All of a sudden, this older lady appeared to fall to the floor so I jumped to my feet to help. Then I saw what she was doing ......

She was on her hands and knees with a putty knife scraping gum off the floor under the table.

Now, let me ask you a serious question.

Do you think that when she was *your* age, she ever considered she would be working like this at *her* age?

Have you ever seen anyone like that? What do you think about that?

If you do things right, that won't be you.

Action Step:

Keep in mind if we're going to help you create an income stream for you down the road for financial security, we need to focus on these 4 things for the Formula for Money NOW Safely:

1) Amount you can save
2) Time to grow
3) Rate of return you can get
4) Taxes

What Happened?

Let's look at the last 10 years.

Incomes have risen – for some people.

But, so has inflation (the cost of living).

However, most incomes have not kept up with inflation.

So, people go into debt with credit cards, payday loans, etc.

This results in poor savings habits.

We spend more than we make.

Lack of long-term security sets in.

Security goes out the window.

Remember that sobering statistic?

Out of 100 people turning age 65 today,

Only 4 are financially secure.

What age are you now?

I guarantee you won't know what the cost of retirement is going to be when you reach age 65.

Is that important to plan for?

You may need to make some concessions so you're ready for what you need down the road.

The problem is, Americans only save 1.3 percent of their income.

Let me ask you a question, how can folks replace 100 percent of their income if they're only saving 1.3 percent of it as they go along? It's almost impossible.

Action Step:

Make a decision today to reflect on your own situation and to take positive steps to improve your destiny.

So What?

Now let's look at the outcome of all this.

Social Security, 401ks, IRAs, rental properties and your various accumulated savings bonds, term deposits and gold coins will likely barely cover basic essentials at retirement.

The majority of companies no longer provide their employees a pension due to the cost and liabilities.

Most Americans are familiar with Social Security which is a U.S. government program established in 1935 to include old-age and survivors' insurance, contributions to state unemployment insurance, and old-age assistance.

The program's Old-Age, Survivors and Disability Insurance (OASDI) trust fund is projected to be exhausted by 2033.

That means if you're expecting to draw upon it, you may not be able to.

So, it's wise to plan for your retirement without expecting Social Security.

The age when a person becomes eligible to receive full Social Security retirement benefits (the full retirement age) has been increasing from age 65 on a schedule set by Congress in 1983. It has reached 66 and will gradually rise to 67 for those born in 1960 and later.

Let me ask you another question.

We talk about the people who want to be financially secure.

I said out of 100 people turning 65 today, only 4 are financially secure.

Do you know anyone who *is* financially secure? What's their life like?

What about people in the 96 percent – what is *their* life like?

So where do YOU want to be?

The purpose of this book is to help you achieve your goals.

Action Step:

Make a decision to let go of any limiting belief and resolve to start thinking seriously about the fate of your future self – especially as we are generally living longer these days.

The Sky Is Falling!

Here's another statistic that is pretty shocking:

A third of Americans are delinquent in debt.

77 million Americans are now in debt collections with the average amount being $53,850.

A third of Americans delinquent on debt

AMERICA'S DEBT LOAD 77 Million Americans Are Now In Debt Collections.
AVERAGE DEBT BY STATE

NATIONAL AVERAGE: $53,850

WASH. $73,380
ORE. $60,752
MONT. $53,171
IDAHO $58,059
N.D. $49,039
MINN. $67,652
MAINE $53,095
WYO. $55,914
S.D. $51,120
WIS. $51,940
N.Y. $51,472
NEV. $51,226
UTAH $62,969
NEB. $46,776
IOWA $46,626
MICH. $43,377
PA. $50,615
CALIF. $69,697
COLO. $74,340
KAN. $45,236
MO. $47,214
ILL. $42,183
IND. $44,183
OHIO
W. VA. $33,970
VA. $74,279
VT. $57,816
N.H. $67,805
ARIZ. $55,831
N.M. $46,497
OKLA. $38,639
ARK. $37,162
KY. $40,309
TENN. $42,378
N.C. $47,516
MASS. $73,156
R.I. $57,700
S.C. $45,756
CONN. $70,591
TEXAS $40,757
LA. $38,077
MISS. $31,065
ALA. $38,784
GA. $46,668
N.J. $67,398
DEL. $60,199
ALASKA $68,524
FLA. $47,181
MD. $76,583
DC. $65,532
HAWAII $83,810

$31,065 TO $45,756 $46,497 TO $53,353 $55,831 TO $69,697   MORE THAN $70,591

That debt could include student loans, credit card debt, car loans, mortgages, medical bills and so on.

Why did that happen to them?

Well, over the last few years, the cost for food, shelter, and transportation as well as the tax rates have all skyrocketed, while wages have fallen.

The average person is making less today than they did 10 years ago and yet things cost more.

Saving money seems like the impossible dream in today's economy.

And yet, there are solutions that are available by using various government-sponsored programs that enable you to save money tax-free and have income for life tax-free.

But you need an open mind – particularly if you're under age 35. ☺

The U.S. government developed a powerful and safe wealth creation system working with the biggest financial institutions in the world.

These financial institutions have billions of dollars in assets and have been in business for decades – some for over a hundred years.

And you can easily become wealthy – doing absolutely nothing of any effort.

Just simple stuff wealthy people do every day.

We discuss those in detail in the **Money NOW Safely** book series and on my website at www.MoneyNowSafely.com

Action Step:

Decide today to become a life-long scholar and take control of your self-education to improve your financial destiny.

Wise Advice

Consider this advice from people you may have heard about.

"The Philosophy of the Rich and Poor is this:

The Rich invest their money and spend what is left.

The Poor spend their money and invest what is left."

That was said by **Robert Kiyosaki** in his book called "Rich Dad Poor Dad"

Have you heard of **Warren Buffett**?

He is now one of the richest men on this planet but he started out as just a regular kid growing up in Omaha. Now he owns Geico, Denny's, Burger King, Kraft/Heinz and a whole slew of other major companies.

For a great book about him, read "The Snowball: Warren Buffett and the Business of Life" by Alice Schroeder, that gives insight into his life and path to amazing financial success.

Here is a famous quote by Warren Buffett:

"I think the biggest mistake is not learning the habits of saving properly early. Because saving is a habit,"

And he also said;

"It's pretty easy to get well-to-do slowly. But it's not easy to get rich quick."

And yet we all dream of buying that winning lottery ticket instead of having a practical plan to become wealthy.

We've all seen people who were wealthy in bankruptcy today.

And retired people working in lesser jobs to make ends meet.

All because of inadequate savings methods earlier in their lives.

The Top 1 percent of people in America with $2 million or more qualify to speak to a financial advisor. The other 99 percent have to figure it out by themselves.

My experience as a banker, stockbroker, financial services provider and business owner enables me to give you the insight and tools you can use to reach your financial goals safely.

Action Step:

Evaluate your advisors as to their ability to help you succeed in your financial well-being.

.

Problem 96% Of Us Have (And Don't Know)

The sooner you identify a problem...the easier it is to fix it!

To be financially independent, you need to know where your money is REALLY going.

Would you agree?

Then, you need to make your existing money work better for you and your future.

Agreed?

Any money that's not enhancing your life or future should not be spent, but saved.

Makes sense, right?

The money you save could be used to pay off debt. True?

Particularly high cost debt – like credit cards, significantly reducing expenses.

Maybe we found money you didn't expect!

So where are you spending your hard-earned money NOW?

In Summary: Free up money you didn't know you had by reducing wasteful expenses.

Together, these will improve your life and lifestyle and future! Agreed?

Action Step:

To have more money later on for your future goals and dreams, you need to know where you are spending your money today.

Here is a link for a list of free apps where you can track your earnings and expenditures, so that you can INSPECT what you EXPECT.
http://listoffreeware.com/list-of-best-free-expense-manager-software/

Ancient Math Rule That Applies Today

Let's talk about **inflation.**

Have you heard of the **Rule of 72**? (See more on *Wikipedia.com*)

Let me explain it; it's really easy and interesting.

It's an ancient math rule that quickly calculates how fast money grows.

Whatever interest rate you're saving at, divide that into 72, and it will tell you how many years it will take for your money you save to double.

For example, let's assume your savings are growing at 4 percent annually.

72 divided by 4 equals 18... So, every 18 years your money will double at 4 percent interest.

$100 earning 4 percent interest would double to $200 in 18 years.

And in another 18 years at 4 percent interest, $200 would double to $400.

Problem... in 36 years from now – will $400 buy what $100 does now?

That same Rule of 72 tells you how fast the COST of things will double.

Over the last 25 years, inflation has averaged 3 percent to 4 percent.

So at 4 percent inflation, the cost of things doubles every 18 years.

For example, consider the cost of a loaf of bread or a gallon of gas.

Let's say bread cost $1 a loaf 18 years ago.

Today, it would cost $2 and then it would double to $4 in another 18 years from now.

The same Rule of 72 applies to the cost of gasoline or clothing or anything else you buy.

That's inflation. So, let's see how that will affect you when you are ready to retire.

Action Step:

Decide today to focus on positive ways to reduce your expenses.

Inspect What You Expect

Remember that out of 100 people turning age 65 today, only 4 are financially secure.

"Inspect What You Expect" means you need to look at where your money is going and how much extra income you will likely need to have available to supplement your retirement income.

We'll ask **5 Quick Questions** to help get you there.

Let's go through an example together to calculate your **Financial Gap** at Retirement.

Email me to get your Free worksheet to calculate your Financial Gap or simply write on something handy.

Let's start out by entering your name and today's date at the top of the page.

Question 1: What age are you now? Let's say you are age 30 today.

Question 2: What age do you anticipate "Retiring" or spending more time on your hobbies? How's 70?

Okay - you have 40 years to earn money until your retirement. (Age 70 minus 30 = 40 years)

However, we're all living longer and the average age expectancy is creeping up to age 90. So if you plan to retire at age 70, you need enough money to fund your lifestyle for at least another 20 years afterward.

So you may wonder – how much money do you need to save to last you for 20 more years at retirement?

Your Current Basic Living Expenses:

The quick and basic calculation is to look at your **Basic Living Expenses = Shelter (rent / mortgage), Food and Transportation.** Money to stay alive but not including entertainment.

Question 3: Roughly how much do you spend on **Basic Monthly Living** expenses monthly now? Say $2,000

Now let's apply the **Rule of 72** using a **4%** inflation rate. (Divide 72 by 4 percent = 18 years) This calculates the number of years to double your expenses.

With inflation at 4 percent; in 18 years from now, you'll need $4,000 a month for what $2,000 does today.

At that time, your age will be 30 + 18 = **48**

In another 18 years, your age will be 48 + 18 = **66**

So, those $4,000 monthly expenses at age 48 will double to $8,000 monthly at age 66.

You're ready to retire, right?

Of course, in another 18 years, you'll be 66 + 18 = **84** (hopefully, still healthy and agile).

Those $8,000 monthly expenses at age 66 will double to $16,000 monthly expenses at age 84. Yikes!

You still have a few more golden years to enjoy until you're 90.

Your Future Income:

Okay, now let's see how much you will have when you retire in **income** from **Social Security** and **Savings**.

Question 4: How much a month will you get from Social Security when you retire? It depends on the number of years you work and amount you contribute to the fund based on your income.

There are several online resources available to calculate this.

The U.S. Government: https://www.ssa.gov/

Bankrate.com:http://www.bankrate.com/calculators/retirement/social-security-benefits-calculator.aspx

In our example, at age 66, let's say you could receive $3,900 monthly from Social Security.

But if you wait to start collecting until age 70, you'll get $5,600 monthly.

The real question is – will you actually be able to collect your Social Security the way the economy is headed? Better not count on it – this may be a phantom income.

Your *real* resource for income will be your own Savings nest egg.

Question #5: How much have you saved to date? (e.g. Bank accounts, ROTH IRA, 401ks, Mutual Funds, Stocks, Rental property)

Take their market value and deduct any loans against them to get the amount to put into this space. Don't include your primary residence since you cannot use this for income later unless you plan to rent it or use a reverse mortgage.

Okay, of course the Rule of 72 applies to this number. In 18 years at an average 4 percent inflation rate, this number will double.

And, in another 18 years (36 years from now), it will double again. Naturally if you save other money, this would be added to the total but for now, let's just work with what you have saved to date.

In our example, let's say you have saved a total of $100,000 to age 66.

Your Financial Position at Retirement:
Now is the time to find out your financial position at retirement based on the numbers we used here.

At retirement, you should plan on leaving your savings to grow and take no more than 5 percent yearly to live on. Realistically, even 4 percent withdrawals can reduce your principal if you are not earning at least 4 percent on the balance.

If you take out too much every year, you will eat away at your principal and be out of money when you least can afford it. Being age 90 and broke is sad.

So, based on 5 percent withdrawals on savings of $100,000, you'll have $416 to spend monthly at age 70.

($100,000 savings X 5 percent = $5,000 yearly ÷ 12 months = $416 monthly income)

But, hopefully you will also have Social Security income. Let's use the number above of $3,900 monthly.

If you also have other pension income from your job, you would add that here. In this example, there is no pension since few people have one these days.

So, your **Total Available Funds** (Social Security + Savings) to spend monthly at your retirement is $4,316.

Your Financial GAP at Retirement:
Take the total of your **Monthly Income** from Savings & Pensions in 36 years and subtract your **Monthly Expenses** to give you a net number for your **Financial Gap** at retirement.

In our example, at age 66: Monthly Income of $4,316 minus Monthly Expenses of $8,000 = <$3,684>

Hmmm.... This is a negative number. Scary, right?

Let me ask you, on a scale of 10 (being High) and 1 (being Low), how important is filling this Financial Gap to you?

Let's see how we can fill this Gap and add a better lifestyle now and later.

Action Step:
Calculate your estimated Financial Gap at Retirement and decide today to put your plan into action to fill that Gap.

Conclusion

Congratulations on taking the First Step!

This book is your launching point for your life of financial independence.

It captures the WHY you need to be self-sufficient financially to live the life of your dreams.

You probably realize that you really need a solid Game Plan to avoid having to work at retirement age like the 96 out of 100 reaching age 65 today.

Instead, you want to know HOW to be financially independent, like the 4 percent who don't NEED to work, although they can CHOOSE to work.

You are now more prepared to establish a Game Plan to fill your Financial Gap.

OK – let's pause here and review what we have learned so far in this book.

Whew!!

We covered a LOT. We learned about the Problem the 96 of 100 had but didn't know.

We learned about the Rule of 72 – How fast Money Doubles.

As a reminder, just divide 72 by the interest or inflation rate.

Example: 4 percent interest / inflation rate

72 divided by 4 is 18... So, every 18 years your money (or your cost of an item) will double.

$100 would become $200. And in another 18 years at 4 percent, $200 would double to $400.

Then we calculated your Financial Gap at Retirement (that's the extra amount you will need to supplement your income from pensions and savings at that point).

We identified your Current Basic Living Expenses (Shelter, Food, Transportation) + Current Savings.

We netted your Future Expenses from your Future Income.

You found out how much income you will need to have to cover your Financial Gap at retirement.

And it's probably different – maybe even MUCH more than you originally thought.

Scary, right?

The Good Part

Now you have a quantifiable concrete dollar goal to achieve.

Not just a hazy idea of being able to enjoy your Golden Years.

You also have knowledge that 96 percent of your friends don't have.

So you can help them realize that time is not on their side.

They also need to understand and apply the Rule of 72 in their lives and figure out their Financial Gap.

Be a true friend – help them help themselves to become prepared before it's too late for them.

Action Step:

Establish your Game Plan to become Financially Independent and help at least one friend with theirs.

Learning Resources

Thanks again for participating in this first book in the *Money NOW Safely* series. I enjoyed sharing my experience and I hope you learned and profited accordingly.

I promise to read your comments and suggestions and apply them in the ongoing series of *Money NOW Safely* books and courses.

Let's work together to improve your financial security.

Connect with us

 www.MoneyNowSafely.com

 GNichols@SafeWealthCreation.com

 www.facebook.com/safewealthcreation

 https://twitter.com/SAFEsavings

 www.linkedin.com/in/gailnichols

Our Services

Eliminate Debt:

Debt is a problem that millions of Americans face...The Problem is most of us do not have a plan to eliminate it. One of our core focuses is helping people with this problem.

Not only can we show you what the debt you have now is and will cost you over time, but also what it could mean to you and your financial future if you were able to reduce and ultimately eliminate this debt.

There can be an end to the cycle... There is a better way.

We will show you a plan with your current information detailing when you can be out of debt with savings established.

We will help you get a plan in place to get out of debt faster than you ever thought possible as well as a new way to make purchases that keeps you in control of your money.

Email Gail at: GNichols@SafeWealthCreation.com

Don't let this be your scenario.

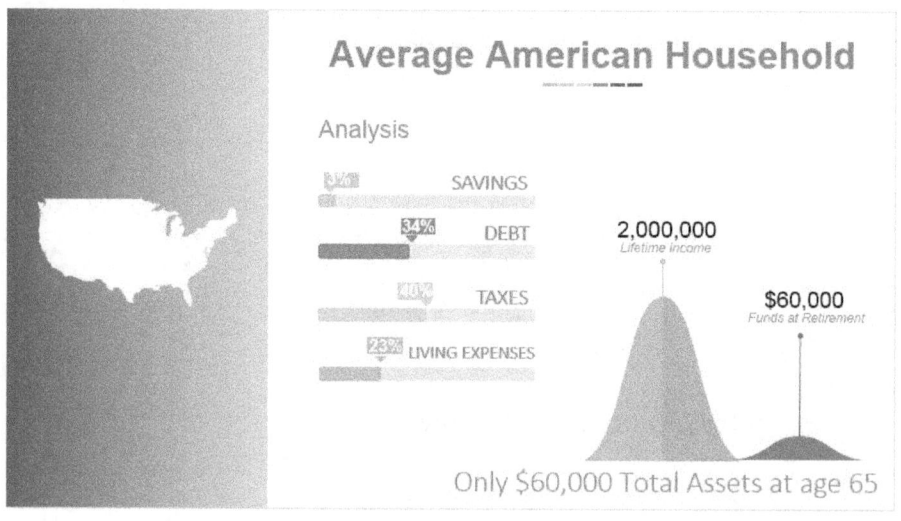

Retirement Solutions:

Do you think that taxes are going to be lower in the future?

Do you think that they are going to stay the same?

Or do you think taxes are going to be higher in the future?

Do you think taxes have to increase if we as a country are going to pay off over $19 trillion in national debt? (Visit: http://www.usdebtclock.org/)

So is deferring taxes really a good idea? Yet what you hear from your CPA and water cooler buddies is that you shouldn't take money out of your IRA because you will have to pay taxes.

THINK ABOUT THIS:

You're going to have to pay taxes at some point...the IRA only *defers* taxes.

At 70½ the government is going to FORCE you take out your Required Minimum Distribution (RMD).

We can show you how to systematically take back control of this ticking tax bomb and create a tax-favored environment not only for you, but also for your family. Email Gail at: GNichols@SafeWealthCreation.com

College Funding & Planning:

Do you have Teens in High School? Do you want the best college for them but you're confused about what financial aid is available or how to prepare them for admission?

We have the answers – join us at a college funding workshop. Schedule one today for your office or group meeting – it's free! Or contact us for a free personal consultation – we're looking forward to helping you.

These days, high school grads as well as their parents view a college education as a "must have" to get a career-worthy job after graduation. But college is an expensive "necessity" and getting more expensive each and every year.

With the cost of higher education rising faster than the cost of inflation, it is estimated that the parents of today's 4-year-olds could face college bills of more than $200,000 per year.

Sure, the numbers are scary, but if you start saving regularly while your child is in diapers, you'll put yourself in a good position financially by the time your son or daughter is ready to enroll. Also, don't forget that the availability of financial aid, loans, and education credits and deductions means you may not have to foot the entire bill yourself.

The problem is that most of us have not done a good job at saving for college. We've known of this impending doom since the day the children were born, but the everyday challenges of life have gotten in the way.

College Planning
Dream Team

Proven. Reliable. Friendly.

That is why our **College Planning Dream Team** is the perfect solution to this dilemma. We provide workshops and personalized strategies for parents to guide them with a proven and reliable system to prepare for and gain admissions to college, including financial aid, admissions assistance, tuition rewards and a customized college blueprint.

FREE College Funding Workshop – What You'll Learn:

• How the **best colleges** can be the **least expensive**.

• How to create the most **efficient** way to pay the college bill.

• How to position your student to receive maximum **merit** money.

• How to get a **$1,000 Guaranteed Tuition Discount** to hundreds of colleges (with the opportunity to get up to **$49,000 in guaranteed tuition discounts** per child - you'll learn how at the workshop).

• How your **529 plan** could cost you thousands of dollars in aid.

• How your kids could go to a top **private** college for less than the cost of a **community** college.

• How to **double or triple your eligibility** for **FREE money** for college.

• How to select a school that will give you the **best** financial aid award.

• How to **protect your Retirement savings & home** while funding college.

• Why governments and colleges keep **funding secrets**.

• The inside story on **Scholarships** + how to **eliminate Student Loan** debt.

• **BONUS:** How to AVOID being punished if you make a comfortable six-figure income and have sizeable assets that can destroy your chances at receiving college aid.

Schedule Your FREE College Funding Workshop:

Email: GNichols@CollegePlanningDreamTeam.com

Visit: www.CollegePlanningDreamTeam.com

Your Business Bank Solutions:

We show business owners how to make their **cash flow** more efficient and **reduce taxes** at the same time.

Every business owner should be in 2 businesses:

1) The business that creates your *REVENUE*.

2) The business that *FINANCES* your business.

➤ Use ONE dollar in more than one place **at the same time**

➤ Use someone else's money for expenditures while yours compounds continuously **eliminating Lost Opportunity Cost**

➤ Gives you **liquidity, control** and **access to capital** with **little to no risk**

We can help you create a source of funds for business expenditures.

You can actually capture excess interest and all principal that you are paying other institutions; and at the same time, create a retirement plan for yourself that is Tax-Free. From petty cash to payroll, funds are continuously moving through your specially designated account.

Whenever a business owner utilizes the advantages of our services, their reliance on financial companies for working capital quickly diminishes. **With time, the business can produce 100% of its financing needs.**

Innovative Retirement Plans For Small Businesses:

Looking to *increase your tax deductions* and prepare for retirement?

Let us help with *Tax-Qualified Plans for Small Businesses*.

Whether you own a restaurant or run your own medical practice, you know expenses can add up fast – including taxes. You have options!

Why Sponsor a Plan?

- Attract and retain quality employees
- Tax-deductible contributions
- Tax deferral on accumulated investment earnings
- Tax-deferred distribution options

Contact us today to discuss. **Email:** GNichols@SafeWealthCreation.com

Financial Education In Your Workplace:

Improving workplace productivity, health and well-being through personal financial education...

PricewaterhouseCoopers' (PwC) **Financial Wellness Survey** reports that 25 percent of employees have financial problems severe enough to have a negative impact on their productivity.

A financially stressed employee spends an average of 20 hours per month of work time on his or her personal financial problems

THERE ARE SOLUTIONS...

We can help your Team (Office, Association, Club, etc.) improve productivity, health and well-being through a **Free Financial Education Workshop** (includes complimentary refreshments).

With No Cost to the Employer or Group Leader, we can:

• Increase Attendees' Income $312 a month on average

• Help them get totally out of debt in 9 years or less

• Help them save at least $300,000 by retirement

• Help them earn up to 49,000 tuition rewards points per child

Schedule A FREE Financial Education Workshop For Your Team.

Email: GNichols@SafeWealthCreation.com

Free No-Obligation Analysis Request Form

✓ Yes! I want to find out how to grow wealthy safely and become my own source of financing for my family and/or my business. Please have an Authorized Money NOW Safely representative contact me so I can receive my free, no-obligation Money NOW Safely Analysis. I understand there will be *no* high pressure and I will *not* be asked to buy anything during this meeting. (NOTE: Please use black ink.)

Name _____

Address _____

City _____ State _____ Zip _____

Day Phone (   ) _____ Evg Phone (   ) _____

Primary Email Address _____

Best time to speak briefly during business hours _____

NOTE: We never trade, rent, sell or abuse your contact or other personal information. By giving us this information, you authorize Money NOW Safely and the Representative we select for you to contact you regarding your Analysis.

Please tell us about you – this will be held in **strict confidence**.

FINANCIAL FREEDOM

	You	Spouse or Significant Other
Age		
Occupation		
Annual Income		
Biggest Financial Concern		
Do you rent or own home?		
Approx mortgage balance	$	Int Rates
Approx credit card balance	$	Int Rates
Do you own a business?		
If yes, type of business		
How did you hear of us?		

FAX this to: 305-460-2230 or **EMAIL:** GNichols@SafeWealthCreation.com

A

BONUS #1

Enjoy reading and sharing other popular books we've written.

Money NOW Safely: Ka-Ching! By Gail Nichols – **Get it on Amazon.com** or via **MoneyNowSafely.com** and **SafeWealthCreation.com**

This book is **Step #2** in a series of books that leads you through the 8 proven, easy and simple steps to achieve financial freedom without stress and pressure.

It's Guaranteed to help you increase cash, eliminate debt, retire wealthy and enjoy life.

Creating safe money habits are effective because they take little time and effort and yet lead you to impressive and satisfying results over time.

For example, in this book you'll learn **why 96 percent of people end up broke and unhappy at retirement age** and how **you can be one of the 4 percent of people who are financially secure way before then**.

Naturally, the sooner you learn how to properly fill your Financial Gap, the faster you'll be financially free!

We'll examine this vital strategy and what impact it will have on improving your life and lifestyle to help you achieve your goals for increasing cash, eliminating debt, retiring wealthy and enjoying life more abundantly along the way.

You'll learn about the amazing **IRS Formula for Success** – that you can instantly apply to improve your financial health. Without knowing this formula and applying it in your life, research shows your likelihood of achieving financial security are almost zero.

BONUS #2

Enjoy reading and sharing other popular books we've written.

The Silver-Bullet Obesity Terminator By Richard Cherry – Get it on **Amazon.com** as well as on **ObesityTheAmericanTragedy.com** and **SilverBulletObesityTerminator.com**

END OBESITY FAST & PERMANENTLY.

Obesity is deadlier than all other causes of disease & death COMBINED.

The heavier you get, the more PAIN & DEPRESSION you have,

Warning you of MAJOR DISEASES developing inside.

This is a Worldwide Pandemic. It's NOT YOUR FAULT.

Virtually all of us started life at NORMAL WEIGHT, Including You.

Yet 74% of us soon became overweight, then 35% became obese GRADUALLY between 1 – 31.

Obesity is 99% caused by – PROCESSED SUGAR – a slow, silent KILLER you actually LOVE.

Diets & Surgery Have Limited Success Because Of The Problem: SUGAR ADDICTION.

Over 50% of all AMBULANCE TRIPS Are Obesity-related.

Written by an experienced Author in a powerful and informative way that you'll enjoy reading.

C

www.ingramcontent.com/pod-product-compliance
Lightning Source LLC
Chambersburg PA
CBHW070422190526
45169CB00003B/1369